LAUGH YOUR SOCKS OFF!

WORLD'S BEST (AND WORST) GROSS JOKES

JESSICA RUSICK

Lerner Publications ◆ Minneapolis

 Did you hear the one about the fart?

 Never mind. It stinks.

Copyright © 2020 Lerner Publishing Group, Inc.

All rights reserved. International copyright secured. No part of this book may be reproduced, stored in a retrieval system, or transmitted in any form or by any means—electronic, mechanical, photocopying, recording, or otherwise—without the prior written permission of Lerner Publishing Group, Inc., except for the inclusion of brief quotations in an acknowledged review.

Lerner Publications Company
An imprint of Lerner Publishing Group, Inc.
241 First Avenue North
Minneapolis, MN 55401 USA

For reading levels and more information, look up this title at www.lernerbooks.com.

Main body text set in Billy Infant Regular.
Typeface provided by SparkyType.

Library of Congress Cataloging-in-Publication Data

Names: Rusick, Jessica, author.
Title: World's best (and worst) gross jokes / Jessica Rusick.
Description: Minneapolis : Lerner Publications, [2020] | Series: Laugh your socks off! | Audience: Ages: 6-10. | Audience: Grades: K-3. | Summary: "What do you call a dinosaur fart? And why did the hero flush the toilet? Learn hilarious jokes that will leave you laughing and grossed out at the same time"— Provided by publisher.
Identifiers: LCCN 2019017999 (print) | LCCN 2019980681 (ebook) | ISBN 9781541576971 (library binding) | ISBN 9781541589070 (paperback) | ISBN 9781541583160 (pdf)
Subjects: LCSH: Wit and humor, Juvenile.
Classification: LCC PN6166 .R87 2020 (print) | LCC PN6166 (ebook) | DDC 818/.602—dc23

LC record available at https://lccn.loc.gov/2019017999
LC ebook record available at https://lccn.loc.gov/2019980681

Manufactured in the United States of America
1 - CG - 12/31/19

Q What's invisible and smells like cupcakes?

A A unicorn's fart.

Knock, knock. Who's there? Interrupting fart. Interrupting fart wh— Pffffffffft!

Q What is the smelliest breakfast cereal?

A Toot loops!

Q Did you hear about the ninja's fart?

A It was silent but deadly.

Q Do cars fart?

A No, but they pass gas.

Knock, knock. Who's there?
Larva. Larva who?
I larva you!

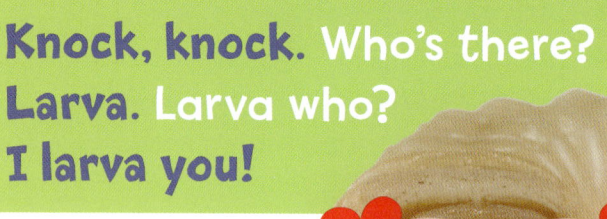

Q What has four wheels and flies?

A A garbage truck!

>>>>>>>>>>>>>>>>>>>>>>>>>>>>>>>>>>>

Q Why did the maggot go to the restaurant?

A To get some grub.

KNEE-SLAPPER

Q What did one fly say to the other?

A Is this stool taken?

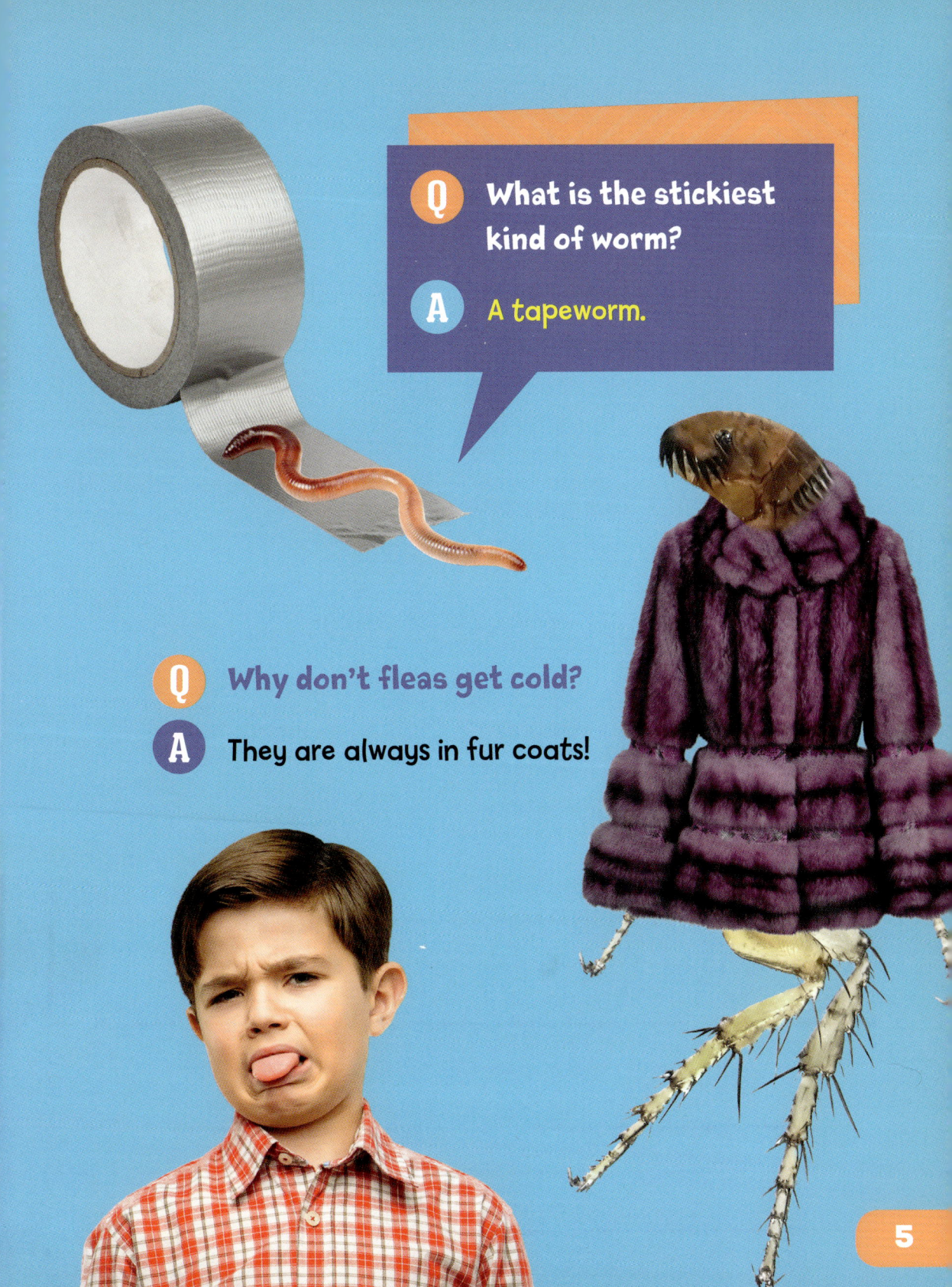

Q Why do gorillas have big nostrils?

A Because they have big fingers!

Q Why do giraffes have such long necks?

A Because they have smelly feet.

Q What do you call a *T. rex* with stinky feet?

A Ex-stinked!

Q What do you call a dinosaur fart?

A A blast from the past!

Q How do skunks get ready for the beach?

A They get spray tans!

Q What do you give a mouse with bad breath?

A Mouse-wash.

7

Q Did you pick your nose?

A No, I was born with it!

Q How do you make a tissue dance?

A Put a little boogie in it!

Q What does someone with a runny nose wear on their feet?

A Tis-shoes!

Q Why was Vera Vomit picked first for the football team?

A She was great at hurling the ball.

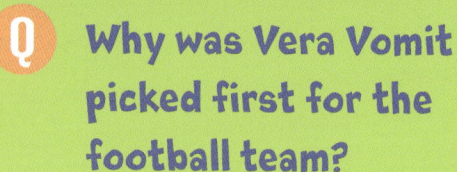

Q What happened when the tornado threw up?

A It blew chunks everywhere.

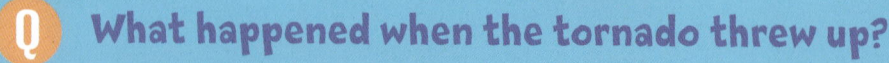

Q What did one piece of vomit say to the other?

A Nice to meet spew.

Q What did the mama vomit say when her son overslept?

A Get up, Chuck!

GROANER AWARD

Q Why is vomit so funny?

A It's always coming up with gags.

Q What is slime's favorite game?

A Slime-on says!

Knock, knock. Who's there?
Slime. Slime who?
Slime to open the door!

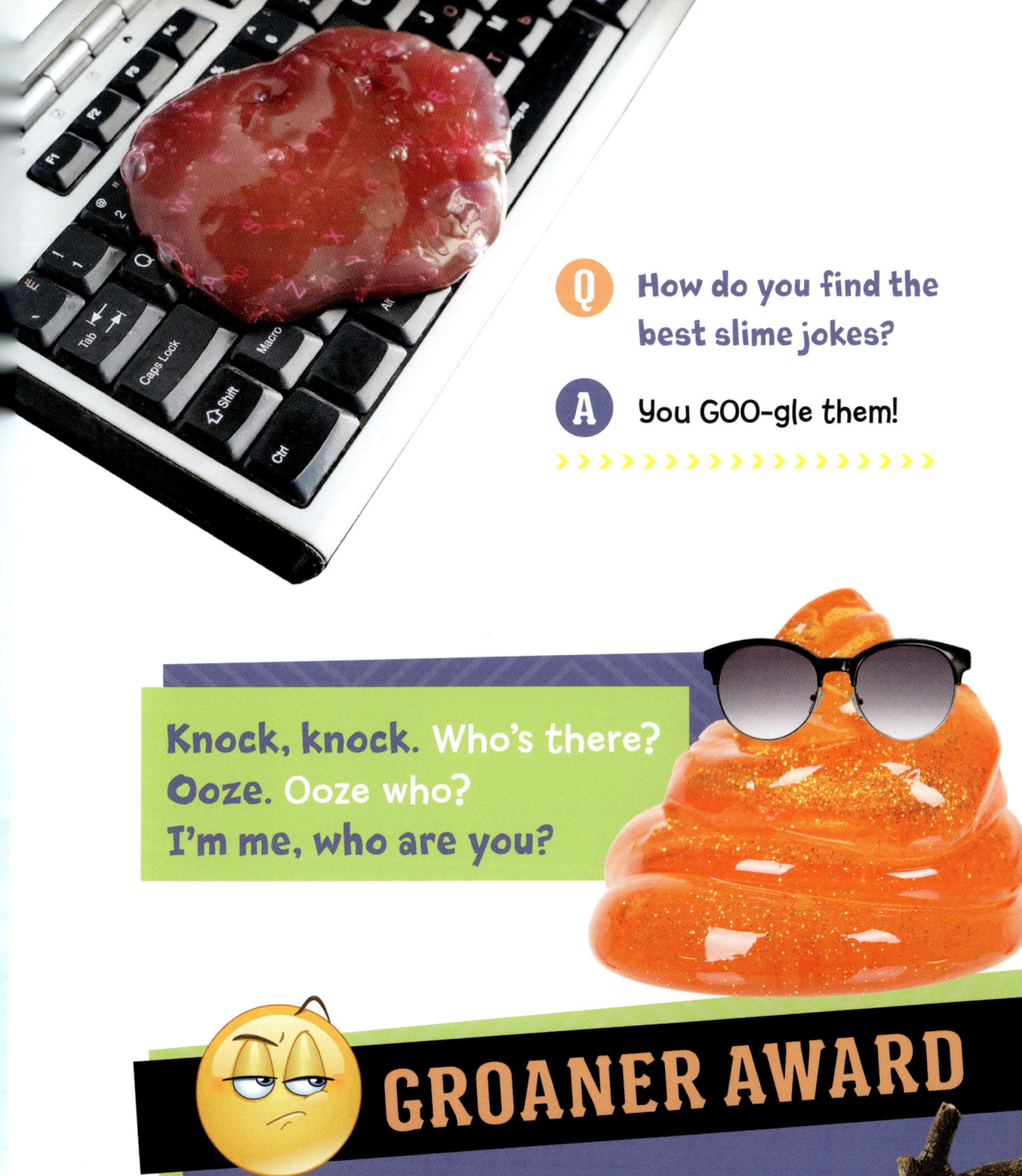

Q How do you find the best slime jokes?

A You GOO-gle them!

Knock, knock. Who's there?
Ooze. Ooze who?
I'm me, who are you?

GROANER AWARD

Q What's brown and sticky?

A A stick!

Knock, knock. Who's there?
I have toop. I have toop who?
You have to poo?
Better get to the bathroom!

Toilet Ted: Tara, are you sick?
Toilet Tara: No. Why?
Toilet Ted: You look a little flushed.

Q Why couldn't the toilet paper cross the road?
A It got stuck in the cracks.

Q Did you hear the one about the green bread?

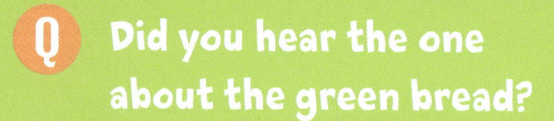

A It's a moldie, but a goodie.

Q What's the difference between roast beef and pea soup?

A Anyone can roast beef!

Customer: Waiter, there's a fly in my soup!

Waiter: The spider in the salad will get it.

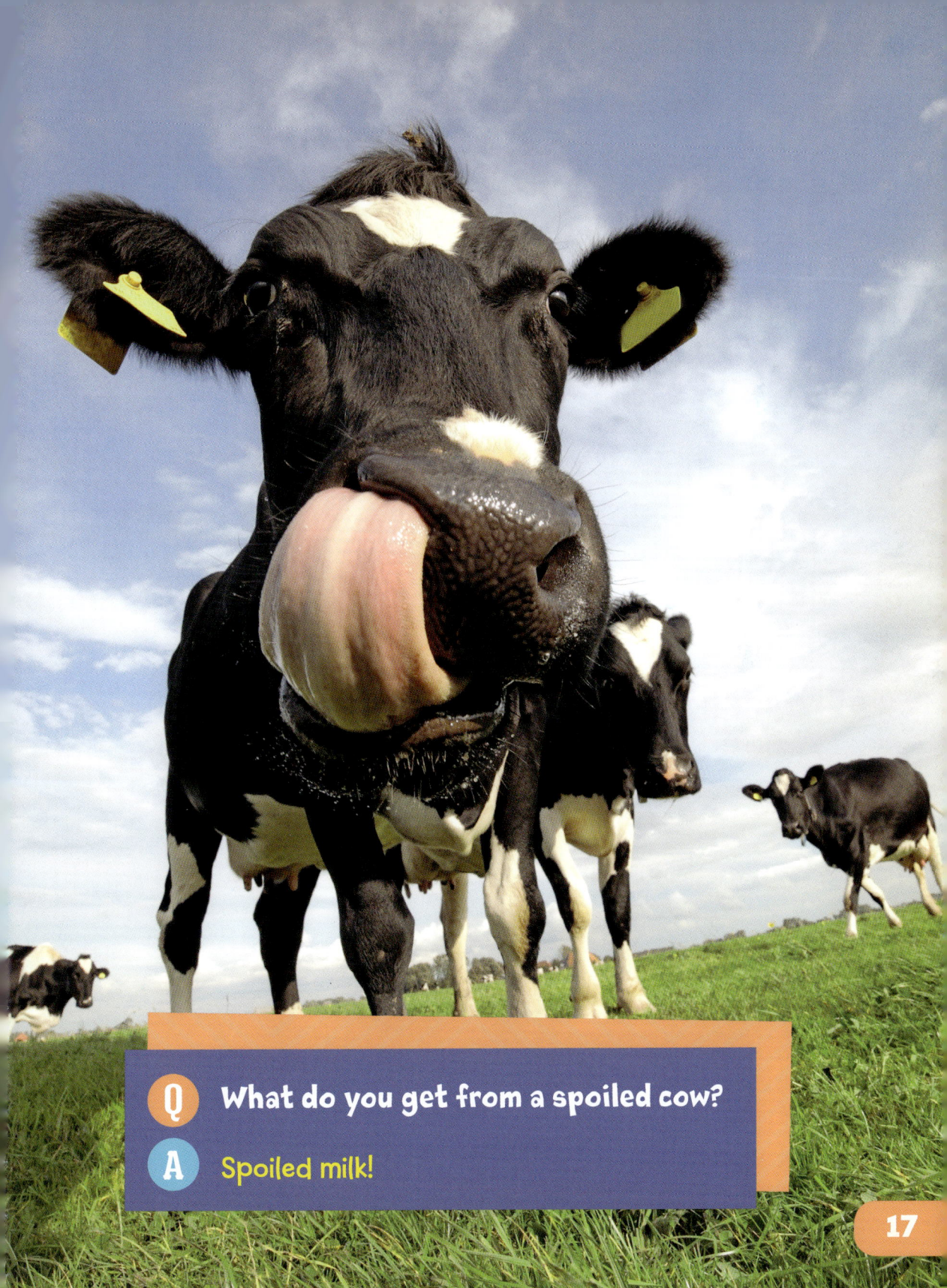

Q What do you get from a spoiled cow?

A Spoiled milk!

Q Did you hear the one about the germ?

A Never mind, I don't want to spread it.

Q Why did the ninja stay home?

A He was sick with the kung flu!

Knock, knock. Who's there?
Ach. Ach who?
Bless you!

Q What is a germ's favorite food?

A Macaroni and sneeze.

Q Why wasn't the computer feeling well?

A It had a virus.

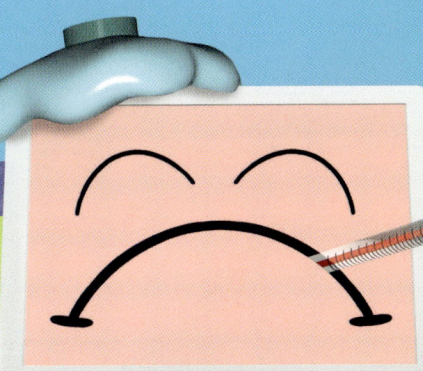

GROANER AWARD

Q What happened when the wind got sick?

A It blew its nose!

19

Q Why didn't the smelly man wear deodorant?

A He didn't have any scents.

Q What do you get when you cross a skunk with a boomerang?

A A smell you can't get rid of!

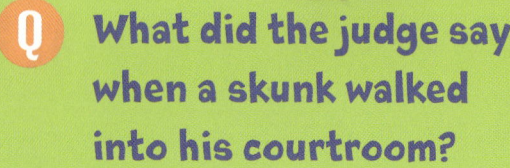

Q What did the judge say when a skunk walked into his courtroom?

A Odor in the court!

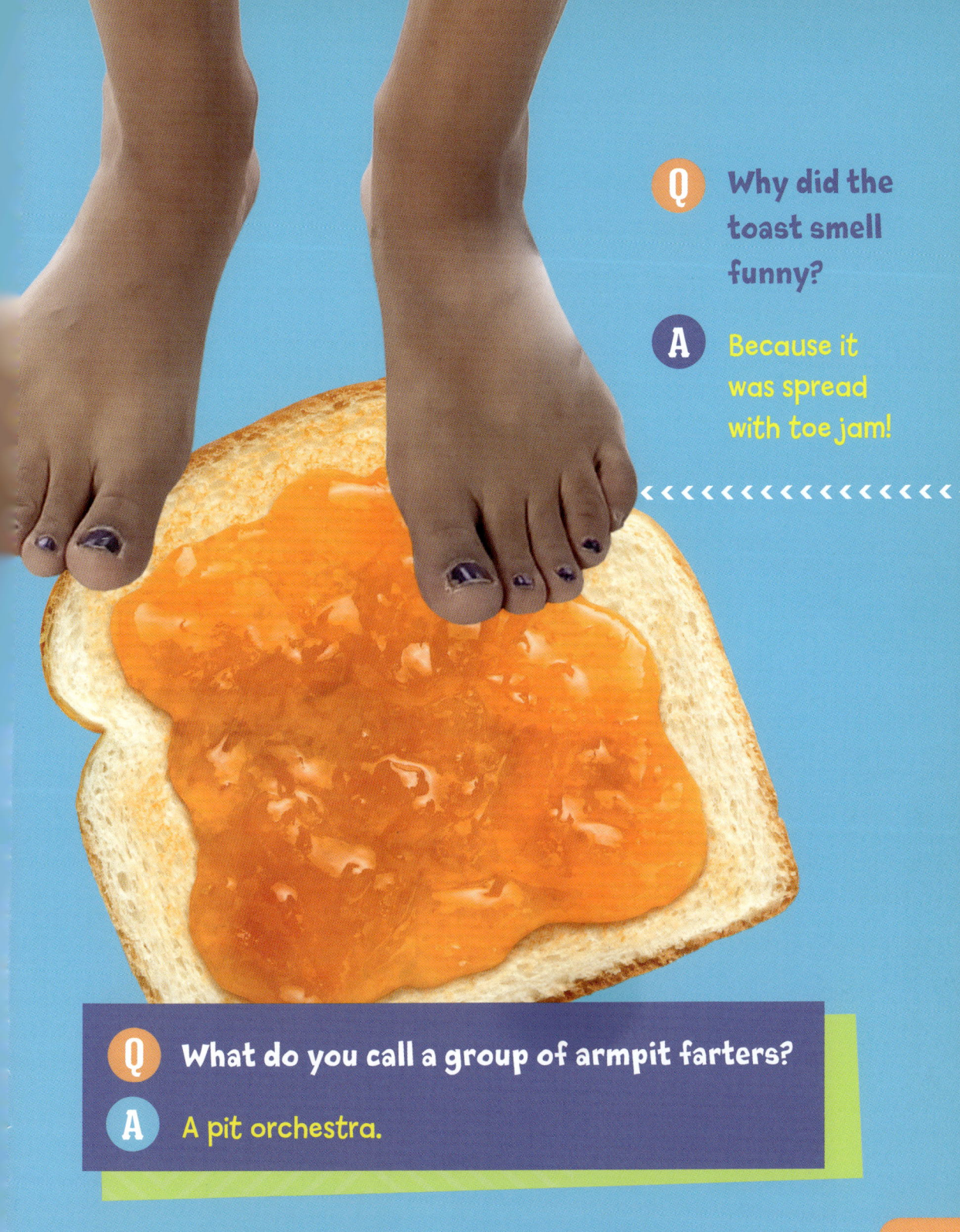

Q Why did the toast smell funny?

A Because it was spread with toe jam!

Q What do you call a group of armpit farters?
A A pit orchestra.

Stan: Are there holes in your underwear?

Stu: No!

Stan: Then how did you get your legs in?

Q What does a storm cloud wear under its pants?

A Thunder-wear!

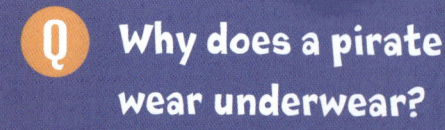

Q Why does a pirate wear underwear?

A To hide his booty!

Q What happened when the butt got embarrassed?

A Its cheeks turned red.

Q What is a butt's favorite food?

A Wedgie salad.

KNEE-SLAPPER

Q Why do ducks have tail feathers?

A To cover their butt quacks!

23

Q Why are butt jokes so popular?

A Because they crack people up!

The images in this book are used with the permission of: Anna Violet/Shutterstock.com, pp. 2 (stink clouds), 3 (stink clouds), 4 (burger), 7 (stink clouds); metamorworks/Shutterstock.com, p. 3 (ninja); Rawpixel.com/Shutterstock.com, p. 3 (car); Zoran Milic/Shutterstock.com, p. 3 (unicorn); dabjola/Shutterstock.com, p. 4 (larva); Tony Oshlick/Shutterstock.com, p. 4 (poo and flies); Aaron Amat/Shutterstock.com, p. 5 (boy); Anteromite/Shutterstock.com, p. 5 (duct tape); hsagencia/Shutterstock.com, p. 5 (worm); Karkas/Shutterstock.com, p. 5 (fur jacket); Protasov AN/Shutterstock.com, p. 5 (flea); Memo Angeles/Shutterstock.com, p. 6 (giraffe); Shay Yacobinski/Shutterstock.com, p. 6 (gorilla); Eric Isselee/Shutterstock.com, pp. 7 (skunk), 20 (skunk); JIANG HONGYAN/Shutterstock.com, p. 7 (dinosaur); PK.Phuket studio/Shutterstock.com, p. 7 (sand); Rudmer Zwerver/Shutterstock.com, p. 7 (mouse); Sorapop Udomsri/Shutterstock.com, p. 7 (mouthwash); Suphatthra olovedog/Shutterstock.com, p. 7 (hat); Happy Together/Shutterstock.com, p. 8 (boy); OoodySmile Studio/Shutterstock.com, p. 8 (tissue); Rvector/Shutterstock.com, p. 8 (slime, slime in tissue); Gooodwin/Shutterstock.com, p. 9 (girl); larryrains/Shutterstock.com, p. 9 (booger); armo.rs/Shutterstock.com, p. 10 (football); blambca/Shutterstock.com, p. 10 (cartoon men); Fidart/Shutterstock.com, p. 10 (word bubble); Kakigori Studio/Shutterstock.com, p. 10 (girl); Illustratiostock/Shutterstock.com, p. 11 (boy); Saravudh Sudkhaw/Shutterstock.com, p. 11 (background); egg design/Shutterstock.com, p. 12 (slime monster); diy13/Shutterstock.com, p. 13 (keyboard); Nik Merkulov/Shutterstock.com, p. 13 (stick); Slava_Kovtun/Shutterstock.com, p. 13 (orange slime); Daniel Love/Shutterstock.com, p. 14 (toilet); gosphotodesign/Shutterstock.com, p. 14 (toilet paper); Diego Schtutman/Shutterstock.com, p. 15 (toilet cape); gmstockstudio/Shutterstock.com, p. 15 (party hat); Lilu330/Shutterstock.com, p. 15 (seaweed); Nadzin/Shutterstock.com, p. 15 (fish); Top Vector Studio/Shutterstock.com, p. 15 (poo); bonchan/Shutterstock.com, p. 16 (roast beef); BW Folsom/Shutterstock.com, p. 16 (soup); iStock.com/slobo, p. 16 (spider); Martina_L/Shutterstock.com, p. 16 (moldy bread); Skphotographer/Shutterstock.com, p. 16 (fly); vitals/Shutterstock.com, p. 16 (salad); iStock.com/SebastianKnight, p. 17; adriaticfoto/Shutterstock.com, p. 18 (girl); Roi and Roi/Shutterstock.com, p. 18 (germs); Anna Kurzaeva/Shutterstock.com, p. 19 (macaroni); iQoncept/Shutterstock.com, p. 19 (computer); Lorelyn Medina/Shutterstock.com, p. 19 (girl); Elnur/Shuttesrtock.com, p. 20 (man, top); Lisa F. Young/Shutterstock.com, p. 20 (judge); Alan Poulson Photography/Shutterstock.com, p. 21 (feet); Danny Smythe/Shutterstock.com, p. 21 (toast); iStock.com/Czanner, p. 22 (pirate); Khvost/Shutterstock.com, p. 22 (underwear, top); Stock_Up/Shutterstock.com, p. 22 (underwear on the line); Irina Nekrasova/Shutterstock.com, p. 23 (duck); Monthira/Shutterstock.com, p. 23 (backside); Joy Brown/Shutterstock.com, p. 24. Design elements: iStock.com/Chereliss; iStock.com/onairjiw; iStock.com/Teploleta; iStock.com/Terriana; iStock.com/Valerie Loiseleux; iStock.com/yayayoyo; TheRenderFish/Shutterstock.com.

Cover: iStock.com/pagadesign (germ in toilet); iStock.com/pkline (girl); iStock.com/Talaj (poo).

24